CAUGHT IN THE
CROSSHAIRS OF HISTORY

Also by John P. Gawlak:

A Voice In The Village Square

When Memories Nudge You Softly

Stand Up To Political Ballyhoo
Plus
Milestones And Memories

CAUGHT IN THE CROSSHAIRS OF HISTORY

THE DEPRESSION, WWII, POST-WAR ADJUSTMENT AND REDEMPTION

John P. Gawlak

CAUGHT IN THE CROSSHAIRS OF HISTORY
THE DEPRESSION, WWII, POST-WAR ADJUSTMENT AND REDEMPTION

iUniverse books may be ordered through booksellers or by contacting:

iUniverse LLC
1663 Liberty Drive
Bloomington, IN 47403
www.iuniverse.com
1-800-Authors (1-800-288-4677)

Because of the dynamic nature of the Internet, any web addresses or links contained in this book may have changed since publication and may no longer be valid. The views expressed in this work are solely those of the author and do not necessarily reflect the views of the publisher, and the publisher hereby disclaims any responsibility for them.

Any people depicted in stock imagery provided by Thinkstock are models, and such images are being used for illustrative purposes only. Certain stock imagery © Thinkstock.

ISBN: 978-1-4917-3545-9 (sc)
ISBN: 978-1-4917-3546-6 (e)

Library of Congress Control Number: 2014909121

Printed in the United States of America.

iUniverse rev. date: 06/11/2014

PRODUCTION ASSISTANCE
Carol Gawlak
Charles Gawlak
Casey and Jennie Gawlak
Catharine and Vincent Paradiso

COVER
John P. Gawlak, the author, at age 16.
He would join the U.S. Navy a year later at age 17.

For my twin sister, Helen (Babe), who endured tuberculosis confinement at a young age, and the early death of her husband, Artie, from which she never recovered.

"Among the beautiful pictures that hang on Memories Wall, is one of my twin sister. That seemeth the best of all "

Alice Cary

"For steel to be true, it must pass thru the fire."

From the novel ***David Copperfield***

By Charles Dickens

"Man may stand while the river flows past, but man will change the river, never."

Author Unknown

<u>Homecoming</u>

Is there a more beautiful sight than seeing the Golden Gate Bridge shrouded in fog after three years of war? Then seeing my family shout with joy when I came through the door? Then heading to the local tavern with my four brothers who beat me home, to celebrate their kid brother who made it back? Then that tipsy singing journey back home when the tavern closed?

Contents

Foreword

This is a story of a young boy struggling during the Great Depression, caught up in WWII, and lucky enough to head home when hostilities ended. Fortunate to take advantage of the G.I Bill, to become a Physical Education Professional, conclude a career with the Y.M.C.A., and be part of the birth of the Middle Class. Our character was forged by struggle and hardship. We never experienced the economy of abundance. Deprivation was our lot. The Depression was a stark, depressing, poverty—laden existence that showed no immediate recovery for better times. It was a long, unpromising time. Winters were severe with long spells of zero weather, and summers, extended heat spells. Homes had no central heating or air conditioners. A coal stove in the kitchen provided heating. Bedrooms were so cold, our beds contained three foot quilts stuffed with feathers. Rattling windows were lullabies that put you to sleep.

When the war in Europe broke out, our economy began to stir with war production, and offered a ray of economic sunshine. But, no sooner when the improving economy brightened our lives, the war broke out and we were all called up to the armed forces. Being the youngest, I would have to wait a year before I could join my four brothers who already were in combat zones overseas. I walked out of my high school one day and joined the Navy at age 17. Soon, I was in the South Pacific aboard the U.S.S. Whitney where I would miss seeing my brother Paul with the 1st Cavalry Division in the Admiralty Islands, and my brother Stan aboard the heavy cruiser U.S.S. Vincennes in the Philippines.

My ship was in the Leyte Gulf, gearing up to invade the Japanese Mainland when the war ended. When President Harry Truman was given a report as to the high amount of casualties we would incur in the invasion of the Japanese Mainland, he gave the order to drop the Atom Bomb that ended the war. I had the option to stay with my ship to join the occupation forces in Tokyo Bay, or head home. No need to ask what choice I made. It took us 21 days to get home on a transport. Twenty-one days of chow lines, playing pinochle, observing flying fish, and dreaming of home. Finally, the sight to make your heart dance, the Golden Gate Bridge shrouded in fog. A 30-day leave, a few more months of service, then back to civilian life. I will write about coming home, years of adjustment to civilian life, a college education under the G.I Bill, getting married, raising a family, and retirement years. The G.I. Bill offered the opportunity to higher education and a better life.

The Family

Polish Immigrant Parents, Two Sisters and Six Brothers

My Twin Sister "BABE"

I had two sisters, my twin sister, Helen (Babe), and an older sister, Ann (Nell). I don't recall much of our early childhood, but we played together, went to school together, and swam the Connecticut River together. My parents were Polish immigrants. My mother was named Mary, and my father, Frank. Polish was spoken in the home. My father was a weaver, but my mother ran the home, and administered whatever discipline was necessary. We attended a Polish parochial school taught by the Felician Order of Nuns. Every morning before class, we met in the schoolyard, and then marched in order to our nearby church for Daily Mass. Then, marched back to our school for teaching and study. Before class began, we sang the Polish National Anthem in Polish, and our Country's National Anthem in English. When we graduated Eighth grade, we were bilingual. We could read, write, and speak Polish and English very fluently. Let me regress a bit, as I have to report some interesting anecdotes of attending school with a sibling.

We lived on the banks of the Connecticut River, which was the source of much of our recreation and adventures. Many of us had our own small rowboats that we fished, hunted, swam, and raced each other. I would often fake illness so that I could skip school and take my boat to fish in warm weather. Well, the nun that taught our class caught on to my shenanigans and would send my sister, Babe, to bring me back to school. By the time she found me, and brought me back to school, classes were letting out. I was reprimanded by my Nun and made to stay after school to catch up on the lessons I missed. I also had to sweep the classroom and wash the blackboards before I was allowed to go home. Discipline was harsh when we stepped out of line or disrespected the nuns. Punishment was stringent: Whacks by a ruler. When our parents found out, we were punished; we received more whacks and a reprimand not to offend the nuns. Upon graduation, there were no Catholic High Schools, so we had to attend the Public School. Middletown was a small town, so we walked to school. Sometimes we would roughhouse on our way to school and come late. Coming in late meant we had to go see the Assistant Principal named A.A. Johnson. One time, one of our group told the Principal we were only a couple of minutes late. His reply was: "How would you like to hang for a couple of minutes?" We were never late again.

Intellectually, we were superior to most public school kids, but we never flaunted that advantage. I misbehaved in Miss NeJako's English class once. She berated me saying, I could never live up to the intellectual level of my sister, Nell. She was really calling me a Dumbbell.

The war would break out and many of us would leave school to join the Armed Forces before we graduated. I joined the Navy and was home on a 7-day leave after finishing Boot Camp. I would attend my Classes' graduation, but didn't stay long because they seemed like children to me. Getting back to my sister, Babe, the brothers and myself were already overseas. Coming home from Sunday Mass, Babe would start vomiting blood. My oldest brother, Walter (Bud), who did not get drafted, took Babe to the emergency room, where she was diagnosed with Tuberculosis and admitted to UNCAS-On-Thames, a TB Sanatorium in Norwich. She would lose a lung to surgery, and after years of recovery, would come home after all the brothers returned from the war. Tuberculosis was rampant at that time. My mother would die from it at another Sanatorium, Undercliff, in Meriden. All of us were in combat situations overseas *and none of us could come home for the funeral.* My older brother, Walt (Bud), would be deferred because of a spot on his lungs, which meant it would have been six brothers from one family at war. We were grateful because he was left to watch over our father and two sisters while we were away.

After the brothers returned from the war, Babe was fully recovered and allowed to come home. The older sister, Nell, would soon marry, so it was left up to Babe to care for the home. The brothers would also drift off to marry, leaving my father and one of the brothers to care for Babe. I would leave to attend The University of Florida under the G.I Bill. The remaining brothers would pool their resources and buy a home out by the lake, moving out to a country setting. My father would soon pass away. You can't forget the day we buried him, because it was the beginning of one of the biggest blizzards to hit Middletown. Babe would soon marry, but it turned out to be a sad and tragic time. Her husband, Artie, would soon die of pulmonary consequences at a young age, leaving Babe in a permanent stage of grief from which she never recovered. After years of grieving, she would succumb to the aftermath of her Tuberculosis surgery and the onset of cardiac disease. Nell would soon die of cancer. It was left to me to bury my two sisters and remaining brothers. I am the last of the Gawlak's standing, but my children, three sons and a daughter have produced twelve grandchildren, so the Gawlak name will live in perpetuity.

My Sister Ann, Better Known as "Nell"

Nell was the older sister, who had the responsibility of looking after Babe and I when we were young. Nell was soft spoken and never yelled at us when we misbehaved. But, when she spoke, we would quiet down and follow her directions. How could I forget the example she set when we were in High School? Whenever I misbehaved in Miss NeJako's class, she would angrily reprimand me saying, "You will never live up to your sister, Ann. She is so much smarter than you and never misbehaves." I give Nell credit, because she never told our mother whenever such occasions arose in school. While in Grammar School, Nell and Babe never had inclinations to become Nuns, as many other girls did. Nell would write letters to me while I was away in the Navy, during the war, informing me of news of home or in town. The saddest letter I ever received was Nell's describing our mothers' funeral. It is too sad and heart breaking to recall. Being in the South Pacific, there were no opportunities to spend our monthly paychecks, so I would send them home to Nell, who deposited them in a bank account in my name. After three years, it was a nice cushion to have when I came home. Nell would help me adjust to civilian life when I came home from the war. She would get married to a returning local soldier, and left the housekeeping to Babe. Nell never had children, and would come down with cancer that was terminal. Her husband, Wally, was like family, but he was so distraught he could not make arrangements for Nell's funeral. So, I took the responsibility and handled all the funeral arrangements. Spouses of Veterans are now allowed to be buried in a veteran's cemetery. I made the arrangements and gave the eulogy for my sister. We would visit her husband, Wally, quite frequently until he passed away and was buried alongside Nell in the veteran's cemetery. Nell always had a cat as a pet, and raised flowers to distribute to her neighbors.

Walter, The Oldest Brother, Better Named "Fisher"

The oldest brother, Walter, nicknamed Fisher would find work in a bakery across the street from where we lived during The Depression. He worked the midnight shift. When we awoke in the morning, he would leave a large bag of day old bakery goods (bread, rolls, cookies, pastries) on the back porch. This not only sustained the family, but, also, the neighborhood kids who attended school with my sister and me. He got the nickname Fisher because he loved swimming in the Connecticut River so much, he wouldn't come home for supper. My mother would send me to fetch him, but he ignored my calls and kept swimming. As he got older, he was quite the neighborhood organizer. He would get local merchants to sponsor the neighborhood football and softball teams. The merchants would fund uniforms that carried their names in front and South End A.C. in back. The colors were blue and white. The sponsors also supplied transportation as they played teams throughout the state. I still have my team pictures. As a youngster, I was the water boy for the football team, and the batboy for the softball team. The war came along and they all got called up into the service. We, the younger generation, would form new teams when the war ended. Fisher loved going to see Yale play football in the Yale Bowl on Saturday afternoons. This was during the Depression, and Yale was a nationally ranked team that produced many All-American players. He would take me with him to see many games. The Yale Bowl seated 80,000 and was filled whenever they played. The most spectacular times were seeing The Cadet Corp. march into the stadium at Half-Time when they played Army and Navy. When the war broke out, all the brothers got drafted except for Fisher because he got deferred for having a spot on his lung. My mother was confined to a Tuberculosis Sanatorium at the time. There was a concern that "Fisher's" spot was also Tuberculosis, but it turned out to be a common infection that was easily cured. Fisher being deferred made it easy for me to join the Navy at 17, so that I could join my other brothers. Coming home on leave from Boot Camp, I would visit my mother in the Tuberculosis Sanatorium. I could never forget how she recoiled in fear and began to sob seeing her youngest in uniform. I would never see her again as she died a year later when all the brothers were overseas in combat situations. It was a blessing Fisher was at home to manage the family after my mother passed away.

Joseph, Better Known As "Rusty"

Rusty got his nickname when he stepped on a rusty nail and he hobbled all summer. Getting medical attention for the indigent during The Depression was uncommon. However, the Polish community was serviced by a Polish doctor, who would make house calls when needed. He treated Rusty so that the infection would not flare into something more serious. Rusty had an aversion to attending school, and was happy to join my father as a weaver when he turned 16. He was a great softball player, and was a star on his team, The "Weavers" in the company softball league. When I was a student at the University Of Florida under the G.I Bill, Rusty decided he had enough of winter weather and decided to move to Florida. On his way down, he stopped at The University, got me out of one of my classes to tell me of his plans. We went to a local tavern to have a few beers. After a while, he began to talk about his war experiences that he never mentioned before. He talked about how he loved gripping the machine gun on his vehicle and mowing down the enemy. But, he griped about being pressed into the Graves Division after the Battle Of The Kassarine Pass. His job was to document and collect dog tags from the battlefield dead. He was wounded in North Africa and was a patient quite frequently at Local Veteran's Hospitals when he returned home. He would write me quite frequently from Florida, letting me know how he was doing. But, as time went by, his letters became disjointed, indicating he was on the verge of senility. I didn't hear from him for about a year. I called the Police Dept. in the city where he lived, but they couldn't trace him because his address was a post office box number. After the war, I had corrective surgery done at the Rocky Hill Veteran's Home And Hospital. I also knew Rusty worked there in the boiler room for a while. I went to see the Director of the Hospital, to see if he could track down my brother's records. He said he had a friend in the Veteran's Records Division and would see what he could find. He was very helpful. He called me in a few days telling me that my brother had died and he was buried in a Veterans Cemetery in Florida. He gave me the exact location and the date he died. (Would you believe it was on Christmas day?) Since I was a graduate of the University Of Florida, my wife and I decided to take a week long vacation to visit my old university, and the Veteran's Cemetery where Rusty was buried. I would visit some of my old professors, and bring home photos of my brother's gravestone and send copies to my other family members.

Pete, The Tramp

The most flamboyant of the brothers was Peter. I don't know how his nickname originated, but it stuck. He was far from what the nickname indicated. He was tall, manly, handsome, and dressed with flair. He was a "Ladies man", and had no difficulty dating the beauties in town. He, too, had no interest in graduating from High School, so he joined my father as a weaver. He was an "outdoorsman", and spent much of his time on his canoe on the Connecticut and Salmon Rivers. He sunned all the time and was quite tanned. He was the most unathletic of the brothers. He tried playing football, but injured his knee and that sent him to the sidelines for good. Pete had an affinity to be a friend and care for the handicapped. Vic Spada came down with Pulmonary Disease and Pete would visit him and take him for walks when he came home for periods of rehab. He would also befriend Ben Kotarski, who incurred Kidney Disease. He would take him in his canoe and fish and sunbathe on the Connecticut River. When the brothers came home from the war, Pete would not go back to work as a weaver. He would take a job with Connecticut Light And Power Company, and became a high-voltage lineman.

Pete would marry, but after fathering a daughter, he left his wife and returned home when she drifted off into many adulterous affairs. We lived in a poor neighborhood along the railroad tracks. When Pete returned home, he and Ragan pooled their finances and bought a newly built home out by the lake. It was our jump from poverty to the middle class. I only lived there in the summer when I came home from college. My father was retired from Russell MFG. Co. and he had a daily routine he was happy with. He would gather the discarded lettuce leaves and vegetables from a nearby farm and produce company and feed all the chickens, ducks, and geese in the neighborhood. Then buy a bottle of beer to drink on the back porch and talk to himself. This made him very happy. When they bought the new house, Pete told Pop it's time to move to a new neighborhood where you can sit in the shade and enjoy your beer. How we judge the needs of people sometimes doesn't mesh with the desires of the people we are trying to help. Pop was so unhappy taking him out of the lifestyle and routine he so loved, that it broke his heart. He went to bed one day and would not get out. I'm sure it was his intent to quickly pass away. But, he lingered for a while and finally got his wish and died. We buried him in the morning that was one of the biggest blizzards to hit the area. Babe would marry and move out. I would marry when I graduated the university and take a job with the Y.M.C.A. in Stamford. That left Pete and Ragan in the home. Pete joined the Merchant Marine and would dodge the Nazi Submarine Packs in the Murmansk Run. When the war ended, his ship was assigned to bring stateside American prisoners who ran away to avoid combat duty in Europe. As the prisoner's were being loaded aboard his ship, he recognized one from our neighborhood. He never told anyone, but on certain occasions, he would angrily curse him when he ran into him in town. Ragan would suffer a stroke that would confine him to the Rocky Hill Veteran's Hospital that would eventually kill him. Pete would also suffer a heart attack that he would succumb to.

Paul, Better Known As "Salt"

Paul got his nickname by the prodigious amount of salt he layered on the tomatoes he was about to eat. He would also leave High School to join his father and his brothers as a weaver in Russell MFG. Textile Mill. He was in charge of the family when it came to dig up the garden for spring planting. I loved this time, as I would gather up the garden worms we turned up to use during the fishing season. He would assign all the brothers areas we had to spade and get ready for planting. Most of the garden was used for planting cabbage and potatoes, but left room for lettuce, cucumbers, tomatoes, peppers, radishes and carrots for daily consumption. There was also a large area for sweet corn. This sustained us during the heart of The Depression. Potatoes and cabbage were harvested in the fall and stored in the cellar for use all winter. My mother would also preserve, in quart sized jars, plums, peaches, pears, and various berries. We also raised chickens, ducks, and three geese. It was eggs everyday and chickens every Sunday. The Geese were reserved for the Holidays: Thanksgiving, Christmas and New Years Day. When the geese became big enough, they would follow me to school, but had to return to the yard when they couldn't cross heavily trafficked Main Street. They would wait in the yard, and when I came home, they would come charging, knocking me down and nipping at me in a display of affection. Salt was the only one not to use the River to swim or fish. He would rather busy himself working in the garden or the chicken coop. He was the least athletic of the brothers, although he would play softball on his company's team. The war came along and he was one of the first brothers to be inducted. He would send home pictures of his training with horses in the First Cavalry Division in Fort Riley, Kansas. But, when they went overseas, the Cavalry was out moded and the horses were left stateside. His Outfit would train in Australia, before being sent to fight in the Philippines, and in New Guinea. He would bring home pictures of a Japanese Flag and an Infantry Rifle he would capture in the

Philippines. He would catch malaria, and when he came home, he would spend many days in the local Veteran's Hospital. When he died, we would bury him in the local Veteran's Cemetery where I would give his eulogy.

Stanley, Nicknamed "Ragan"

I don't know how Stanley got nicknamed Ragan, but he carried that moniker with pride. He loved the River where he swam and fished every opportunity he got. In fact, he is the one who taught me to swim. He instructed me on what to do, then threw me off the dock in deep water. I would follow his instructions (duck paddle) and would become quite proficient when it came to fulfill your right of passage by swimming across the widest section of the river. Ragan did not go to High School. He chose to go to the local state trade school to become a tool and die maker. When he graduated, he took a job with Wilcox-Crittenden, a company that specialized in Marine hardware. The war in Europe was heating up, and his company was called on to supply the U.S. Navy with anchors, chains, and cleats for newly commissioned ships. Two months before Pearl Harbor, he would leave the company and join the Navy. I would also join the Navy and would just miss seeing him aboard a cruiser in the Philippines. As a kid, he would come home one evening with a gaping hole in his left calf. It was a deep wound that needed a doctor's attention. Medical attention was hard to come by during the Depression. My mother would call a local Polish Doctor (Dr. Piasta) who would come to the house and would disinfect and suture the wound so that it would heal properly. Before he joined the Navy, he had a steady girlfriend in the next town (Meriden) named Sally Boncek. I don't know what happened, but Ragan was overseas for years, and when he came home, Sally already married someone else. It broke his heart, and he never sought another girlfriend. Ragan would suffer a stroke, and would pass away from a heart attack while confined in the Veteran's Hospital. I would give the eulogy at his funeral, when we put him to rest in the Veteran's cemetery.

The Youngest Brother Named "Cue"

When school let out, it was a ritual during the Depression that we would all get short haircuts. A neighbor was a barber, and we would all line up in his yard, and he cut our hair for free. When it was my turn, he shaved my head. It shown so brightly, that it gave me the nickname "Cueball", which I shortened to Cue. We played, fished, and swam that River all day. We would sunburn so badly, our backs would blister, and then peel. We also fished the River everyday. It teemed with Pike, Bass, Perch, Eels, and Bullheads. At the end of the day we had a ritual. We would bait our hooks and toss them in one place. Then we would urinate, together, where our hooks were. For some reason, this attracted the biggest perch of the day. By Fall, Carp would start to bite. We would catch 35-pound Carp and sell them to the Jewish market. It supplied us with spending money for candy, ice cream and the movies. The River had a three-foot tide. The River would freeze 3 feet thick. When the tide went out, the ice would settle creating a cracking sound that reverberated around the hills, scaring the hell out of us. In Spring, heavy rains and melting snow up north would make the River rise to flood stage called the Spring Freshet. It was a dangerous time to venture out on that river as it ran heavy, muddy, and fast, carrying all kinds of debris. Shad spawned in early Spring. By the Fall, the eggs would hatch and the young Shad (called Buckies), 3 inches long, started their migration back to the sea. They traveled close to shore in large numbers. There was a brownstone quarry near the river. They would dynamite at closing time, to prepare for work the next morning. The most amazing sight you will ever see was millions of young Shad leap three feet high, simultaneously, when the dynamite was detonated. It was a spectacular sight as they sparkled in the sunlight. When we came home from the war, Eddie Siecienski and I hunted and fished the River together. We kept our rowboat downstream so that we could cross the River and hunt ducks in Rice Pond. One day we found our boat was riddled by .22 bullets. We knew who did it, because the wise guy hunted the same places we did. He also had a boat he kept close to home. Eddie and I got up early one morning, and blasted his boat with our shotguns. Eddie and I still fish the River together. We are in our late eighties, so we will continue until our mobility comes to a halt.

I need to add a few notes about my few remaining days as a sailor. Early in my service I was injured when cargo shifted in heavy seas and pinned me to the bulkhead. I was treated aboard ship, but was told I would need corrective surgery before I got discharged. While in my waning days at Fort Schuyler, I reported to our stations medical officer about my need for corrective surgery. He looked up my record, and after examining me, had me shipped to nearby St. Albans Naval Hospital. While recovering, we were entertained by stars from various shows on Broadway. One day, Gertrude Lawrence, starring in the play The King And I, came to our ward. When she came to my bed, she sang one of the feature songs of her play, "If I Loved You." It was so intense and appealing, that to this day, I feel she made it personal, leaving me feeling she fell in love with me.

<u>That Old Gang Of Mine</u>

There is an old song that goes:
>   *Not a soul around the corner*
>   *That's a pretty certain sign*
>   *Wedding bells*
>   *Are breaking up*
>   *That Old Gang Of Mine*

I believe it is appropriate to start the next section of this book by highlighting how we, as friends, grew up together, went to school together, played ball together, swam and fished and hunted that River together, and went off to war together, came back, married, raised a family, and still get together to recall the Depression, war and redemption.

I am looking at a picture of our graduating class from St. Mary's Grammar School in June of 1939. In September, we would enter Middletown High School. The war was breaking out in Europe, and by 1941, we would also be at war and at that age, where we would be inducted into the Armed Forces and life would never be the same again.

That Old Gang Of Mine Coming Home From The War

Joe Burek (Baker)

Baker would be drafted into the Navy. He was lucky enough to be assigned to a sub chaser stationed in Charleston, South Carolina. He patrolled the East coast, as Nazi subs were plentiful in the area. When the war ended, I came home on a 30-day leave. Baker was home at that time, and we would be invited to help celebrate the burning of the mortgage of the Polish Falcons Fraternal Club House. Many Polish neighbors were there to celebrate with their families. It was there I would meet Sophie L. She swept me off my feet. I would court her for a while, but coming home after three years at sea, I needed some space to also celebrate with many of my friends who were also coming home. This caused many interruptions in our relationship, and we drifted apart, leaving me with many regrets. We were soon discharged from the service, and adjusting to Civilian life was a period of uncertainty that caused me many problems. My mother passed away while I was in the service, combined with corrective surgery I needed at St. Albans Naval Hospital on Long Island. I left High School before I graduated, that left another void when contemplating the future. Baker's mother was concerned about my nutritional needs that I had to have supper at Baker's house for quite sometime. The mother of another close friend had the same concern, so I alternated having supper at their home. Baker took a job with a fruit and produce company next door, and on Saturday, I would help him deliver fruit and vegetables to the many summer resorts in Moodus. I was paid with enough fruits and vegetables to take home. Baker was a very good basketball player on the varsity team of our local high school. When we came home, Baker and I would enter a team in the local Y.M.C.A. House Basketball League. We were very good and almost won the championship. But, it was the River that drew Baker and me as we fished and hunted constantly. Weather was no problem as we fished and hunted in rain, snow, or stormy conditions. It became kind of dicey, when we had to cross the Connecticut River to hunt ducks in Rice Pond.

Late November, the wind would kick up, being heavily clothed and transporting our shotguns, it became risky. Also, when hunters on the other side of the Pond fired at ducks, sometimes we would be rained on by their falling pellets. I would become a laborer in the construction business. Our hangout would be the Hof-Brau Tavern. Frank Budka, the owner, would hold a game day. All hunters would bring whatever game they shot and Frank would cook them all in the same large pot. Baker and I would hunt snapping turtles, and Frank would cook them and serve everybody. The highlight of Frank's cooking would be the Annual Pig Roast. Frank would dig a pit and start cooking a piglet early on a Sunday morning. He would start serving at 2 in the afternoon with the best late Fall sweet corn and homemade chowder you ever tasted. We never drank much during the week, but Saturday night was the time to ward off the pains of digging ditches and carrying loads of concrete. But, Baker took a little longer. He would drink during the week. This would carry over into his decision making for a better life. Reading the newspaper at the Hof-Brau one evening, I ran across an article stating that an opportunity to take advantage of the G.I. Bill would run out in a few months. I convinced Baker that we should apply and take advantage for a better future. I had chronic bronchitis, and my last visit to the doctor told me I would never find relief until I moved to a warmer climate. I told him I would be applying to go to college under the G.I.Bill, and my thoughts were on staying at home. He advised me it was a bad choice with my chronic condition and advised a warm climate site of Florida, Arizona, or Southern California. I decided that going out West, I wouldn't come back home, so I chose Florida. Baker decided he wanted a new start in life, so he chose to join me. I didn't have my high school diploma, as I left school early to join the Navy. But I took the exam for my G.E.D and sent mine in and got accepted, but Baker decided to stay home and peddle vegetables. I would go on to graduate and have a successful career with the Y.M.C.A. Baker would continue to drink heavily, which eventually sent him to the Cemetery.

Ted Kalinowski (Luke)

Luke lived nearby and we went to grammar school and high school together. He never was a good ballplayer, but he accompanied our many games and cheered us on. He was drafted into the Infantry (The Rail-splitters) and was wounded when his company got caught in an open field and was strafed by a Nazi warplane in Germany. He received a bullet in his calf, but recovered and finished the war back with his outfit. I mentioned before that his mother would have him bring me to their home for supper. He had a dog named Luke. I also had a dog named Jake. We would walk the railroad tracks along the River, and the two dogs loved hunting muskrats. One day they caught one and tore it in half. He would join Baker and me when we fished, but all he did was throw rocks at seagulls, trying to bring them down. In Summer, we camped on the Salmon River, where we hunted snapping turtles. A mile up the river, one of the cottage owners would let us refill our water jugs from his well. To repay him, we would give the turtles we caught to him, which he loved to eat. Further upstream, was a famous summer resort named Ted Hilton's. I met my future wife there, who worked as a chambermaid cleaning cottages and making beds. The resort would feature a hot dog roast on Fridays and strawberry shortcake festivals on Sundays. Ted Hilton Senior, the resort owner would be one of the servers. Luke and I would join in with the guests and compliment the owner for the fine resort he had when he served us. They brought in a band on Saturday nights and Luke and I would attend that and dance with the many beautiful women who were there on vacation. There was a high diving board on a float, from which Luke and I would entertain the guests with our many stunts. Ted Hilton, Jr. was in charge of the water activities. He knew we were not guests. We became friendly with him and he let us enjoy the waterfront. Chuck Carpenter's father was a classmate of Ted Hilton Senior and we became friends when he was in charge of horses, which he swam across the river to entertain guests. He would join us at our camp, bringing food from the kitchen, that we repayed by sharing our beer. But the Hilton Family and Chuck's close relationship would end in tragedy. The Senior Hilton would commit suicide by locking himself in his garage with his car running. Ted Junior would get into various forms of trouble before selling the resort and moving to Florida. Chuck would accompany him, and both would succumb to drug overdoses. In the winter we would drive to Bear Mountain Ski Resort in New York. We would sit at the bar, telling women there, what great skiers we were, but are now sidelined by minor injuries. We would laugh all the way home at the reaction of the women we spoke to, While we were attending high school, Luke and I would skip a day in the Spring to go fishing. We were having lunch at Luke's house, when Pat Kidney, the truant officer knocked on the door. Luke's mother would chase him away with a broom, cursing him in Polish. We would part ways when I went off to college and then got married. Luke would work with a local nursery. He would develop heart disease from which he died. We would all attend his funeral when they buried him in the local veteran's cemetery.

John (Speed) Kowal

We called him Speed because of the way he walked: slow and ambling. Speed was late getting discharged from the service. One day he was sitting on the curbstone near the gas station where we hung out. He was still in uniform, wearing his bomber jacket. He handed me a cigar (A Rosedale), which was one of high quality. He said he heard I smoked White Owls, which we could buy in Ship's Store for 50 cents a box. He never talked about his war experiences, as he was a tail gunner on a B-17. We grew up together in the same neighborhood and went to our Polish Parochial School. We met as a group and walked to and from school together. One of the group was a grade older and a wise guy who would push us smaller kids around. I would get into a fight with him, but being bigger and stronger, he pinned me to the ground and wouldn't let me up. Speed would pull him off of me and beat him up. He may have walked with a slow gait, but on the basketball court he was swift and agile. He played Varsity in High School, and would be our high-scorer in the Y.M.C.A. House League. He was a quiet and smart student in parochial school and the Nun's admired and praised his intellect and demeanor. He had some good-looking sisters that I will mention later. Speed and Baker's folks ran a bakery together (K and B Bakery) and Speed would help out when he could. Speed's father would own a truck that he used to deliver goods in the nearby towns. He carried a revolver to prevent hold-ups. When his father passed away, Speed brought the gun when we were fishing on the River. It was old and the bullets were leaching. Speed was afraid to fire it, so I took it and fired all the rounds at a road sign. I was wary as the gun smoked like hell when I fired it. He would take the empty gun and throw it into the River. We would work in the tobacco fields when we were kids in the Summer. During lunchtime, one of the older kids would try to boss us around. He had no right to do that and I got into a fight with him. He was bigger and older, but I held my ground against him. I know Speed was ready to step in if I faltered. Coming home from the war, we would have a few beers on Saturday nights, and then drive to The Polish National Home in Hartford for their regular dance night. We met a few girls who invited us to their home in the next town after the dance. They would treat us to homemade apple pie and coffee. They gave us half of a pie to take home that Speed threw onto the top of a nearby car. My second year at the University Of Florida, someone knocked on my dorm room door. It turned out to be Speed. He decided to enroll and join me. We would go out to play tennis one Sunday afternoon. Being a Physical Education Major, I knew what socks to wear to prevent blisters. He had just bought new brown socks. While playing, he developed blisters on both feet. The dye from his new socks would infect his feet so badly; he had to spend most of that semester in the infirmary. He never came back to the University. We rode home together and visited one of his sisters, who was a model in New York City. She lived with two others and they cooked us a spaghetti dinner, then took us out to see the sights of the City. He took a job with the Post Office and his friends helped him build a log cabin on a hill overlooking the next town. He met a girl that he wanted to marry, but she refused to live in his log cabin. It broke his heart. While delivering mail, he began to stumble. He went to see a few doctors, but they never really diagnosed what he had. He finally went to a specialist, who told him, "For Christ sake, am I the one to tell you you've got Lou Gehrig's disease". It was slow acting, so he continued to work until it became too disabling. I was working in Stamford at the time and came to Middletown to visit my brothers quite frequently. My wife and I would also pay him a visit. When I came to town alone I would visit him, and he would take me for a ride in his old pick-up truck to visit places along the River that were familiar. We were driving down a dirt road along the River once and a huge, black snake started to slither in front of the truck. He stopped the truck and let the snake slither by. I know why. He told me once that he planted a garden to raise vegetables. Well, raccoons would eat much of what he planted, so he decided to trap them. He would shoot some and drive others to the other side of the River and let them go. One day, there was a young raccoon in his trap making funny noises. He got his gun to shoot him. But he couldn't do it. He starts to cry and smashed the gun against the tree and let the raccoon go. He shouts," Get out of here you lucky bastard! I wish I was as lucky as you are" He identifies with the doomed animal, but realizes, luck is not on his side.

Another time, while in town, I picked up a few friends to visit Speed. His cabin was on a hill overlooking the Valley below. He was feeding chickadees that plucked sunflower seeds out of his hand. We brought out some beers and we sat on the porch recalling the funny events we went through together. The longer we talked, the more we laughed, until we cried. Speed would worsen where he would join my brother Ragan in the Rocky Hill Veteran's hospital, who was there suffering from a stroke. My friend Willie and I would visit them weekly, and in warm weather, wheel them outside in their wheelchairs. Their conditions would worsen and both would pass away in that hospital and be buried in the local veteran's cemetery.

John Cubeta (Number 88)

Being Italian, John was unable to attend St. Mary's School with us. He attended public schools, and we would finally be classmates in high school. We attended many classes together, but the one to remember was a study class supervised by Miss Potter, who was very elderly. John and I didn't study much. He was quite artistic and would draw war pictures; especially war planes bombing enemy cities. Both of us were attracted to Rita Ciaburri, who sat a few seats away. John and I would shoot spitballs in her hair that she found amusing, but Miss Potter didn't. She would come to our desks and shout, "See here you two, cut this out and get into your studies." Nothing developed out of that relationship, but when my sister, Babe, got married, their first apartment was in a house owned by Rita's mother. Rita was not married and also lived in that house. Whenever I visited my sister, Rita would come up and join us. It was fun to recall the spitball days. I don't know details, but my sister Babe would inform me that Rita passed away at a young age. In later years, Johnny would become a tremendous football player that got him inducted into the Middletown Sports Hall Of Fame. But, let's back up and relate how it started.

While in High School, Johnny would tryout for the football team, but was not selected because he was told he was too small. The war was going on, so Johnny was so disappointed, he left school to join the Marines. He won the Bronze Star in Iwo Jima. As kids, during the winter, we would build model airplanes and fly them over the Connecticut River, where they fell into the water and drifted downstream. John's father ran a fruit and produce store on Main Street. He would cook raw peanuts in front of the store. The aroma attracted everybody passing by, and they all stopped to buy a bag. The most comical event I saw at the store was when an elderly woman, who was caring for a bedridden gentleman, would shop at his store. Fruits and vegetables were displayed outside of the store. This woman, who the father called a sourpuss, always was angry and mean-spirited. I happened to witness this. She asked John's father for the price of cherries. When he told her, she angrily admonished him that the price was too high and walked away. When she did, John's father began to laugh and said, "Her face is like a bunch of cherries."

John would invite me many times to have spaghetti and meatballs for dinner at his house. You wouldn't eat a better pasta dinner anywhere else. When Johnny came home from the war, he would play semi-pro football with a local team named The Blue Jackets. He was a running back and became so popular, he was offered a scholarship to a Junior College team in California. Things did not go well out there, so he retuned home after two years and would rejoin The Blue Jackets. He would become a butcher and run the meat department in his father's store. I would go off to attend college on the G.I Bill. Both of us would marry, and get together to attend UCONN Football games then go out to dinner. I would come to Middletown quite often to fish the Connecticut River with another friend, Ed Siecienski. John would join us, but he didn't fish. He would paint beautiful landscape scenes that fill my house. John's health would fail and his ability to walk would diminish. His wife would pass away, and a daughter he fathered years ago surfaced and moved in with him to care for him.

Ed Siecienski-Fellow U.S.Navy Vet

Ed did not go to St. Mary's School with us. Although he was Polish, his father sent Ed and his sisters to public schools. Ed and his grandfather fished the Socony Docks near his home. We all did, but I didn't get to know Ed well until we came home from the war. While fishing one day, Eddie's grandfather tied into a fish that was too big to control. He couldn't be stopped when he made a run. The fish made a run to the river's channel. All of a sudden, an oil barge towed by a tugboat appeared and cut the grandfather's line. The best guess of what kind of fish it was turned out to be a sturgeon. It was the talk on that river for years. There were other references to sturgeons by Seine fishermen; catching shad that had their nets torn to pieces.

Eddie and I came home from the war at the same time and we got to know each other a lot better over a few beers at the Hof-Brau Tavern. My friend, Baker, was home at the same time. Baker and I stopped at the Rose Garden for a few beers. In a booth, were three girls with a church counselor. They stopped there for a coke after their weekly meeting. Baker and I went over to join them in the booth. I never got hit so hard by Cupid's Arrow when I saw Eddie's sister, Mary Anne. I tried dating her, but she held me at arms length. Her father was a boot legger and alcohol scared her. She finally told me, "Lips that touch wine, will never touch mine." I didn't give up. When we got discharged, Edie and I would go hunting. I would stop at Eddie's house early in the morning, where his mother cooked us breakfast. Eddie doesn't believe me when I tell him I really didn't come to go hunting; I came to see Mary Anne. She never came down to join us for breakfast, but her two sisters, Ann and Helen did. They would pull my hat off, muss my hair, hug me, and say, "Mary Anne won't go out with you, but we will be glad to go." Their mother would chase them upstairs as they ran, laughing and giggling.

One time when Eddie and I were hunting, we shot a squirrel out of a tree. He landed in deep snow and we never found him. Eddie's father was in the Merchant Marine. When I was still in the Navy, Ed's father and I would catch the same train back to our base in New York City. When Ed and I got discharged, we tried out for the Brass Rail Brewers Softball Team. When we didn't make their roster, we decided to form our own team. We approached Pee-Wee Winner, the owner of the Parkside Restaurant and Bar to sponsor us. Since we were his regular customers, he did. The Brewers colors were green and white. South Enders decided on Red and White. We would play the Brewers for the City Championship. It turned out to be the greatest softball game ever played in Middletown. Ed Mikucki would Pitch for the Brewers, striking out 13, while Ed"Michigan"Wiernasz would pitch for the South Enders, almost matching Mikucki in strikeouts with 9. The game turned in the sixth inning. Mikucki would beat out a slow roller and was bunted to second. Joe Pisa hit a shot that was going directly to our shortstop, Ed Siecienski, but our pitcher stuck out his hand, diverting the hit past our shortstop, for the only run that beat us.

Ed would marry and raise a large family. I would also marry and accept a job with the Y.M.C.A. in Stamford where I raised a family of four children and 12 grandchildren. After retirement, Ed and I would get together again and resume our fishing on the Connecticut River and trout fishing on the Salmon River. We even fish on a warm day in winter. Two years ago we caught trout on a warm day in February. This past October, 2013, I caught a 25-pound carp while a 3-foot pike snapped Ed's line. We can't wait to start fishing again.

Stan Krawczynski-We called Him Harry Craft

Harry was another classmate at St. Mary's school, who was well behaved in school but razed hell on Saturday nights. He wasn't very visible in high school, but left at age 16 to take a job with a machine company in Hartford. He would get drafted into an Infantry Division that saw a lot of action in Europe that he rarely talked about. After the war, when we met at the Hof-Brau Tavern on Saturday nights, he was the only one who came fully dressed with a shirt and tie. We would go to various Polish clubs in the area that sponsored dances on Saturday nights. The group of us would go to the dance floor to try to pick up women on the make. Harry would stay in the bar, get loaded, and sing all the way back home. He learned to play the trumpet, and some Saturday nights he'd follow us home blowing his horn, almost getting us all arrested.

We had a camp on Salmon River in the Summer. Harry and "Foxy" built a small motorboat and would travel down the Connecticut River and join us at our camp on weekends. They not only brought a case of beer, but dozens of sweet corn and the choicest steaks we would cook on the fireplace, and have a grand feast. After a few beers, "Foxy" would break out his guitar and we had a helluva sing-along. They would head home before it got dark and would return the next day and start the festivities all over again.

Harry had a bad back and had trouble sleeping. He found relief by getting half loaded before he went to bed. We didn't drink much during the week because we had to get up early and go to work. We would hang out at the Hof-Brau, play cards or Cribbage, or read the newspapers.

Harry never became a good ball player or cared to hunt or fish. When we played softball or basketball at the Y.M.C.A Harry was always there to cheer us on. Most of us would get married and raise a family, but Harry remained single. Harry was also very devout as he never missed a Sunday Mass or

John P. Gawlak

Holy Days Of Obligation. He never sat in the seating area of the church. He always went upstairs where the choir and organist were, not to sing, but he enjoyed the music. Winters were cold and dreary. After Church, we would meet at Hall's Diner, have a cup of coffee or a bowl of soup, then go home to read the Sunday newspapers, or watch a professional football game, go to bed early, as we had to go to work the next morning. Harry would come down with cancer that eventually killed him. We would all attend his funeral at the local veteran's cemetery.

Lou Haydon

Another of our neighborhood who attended St. Mary's, Middletown High School, and leave early to join the Navy, was Lou. After the war, we talked about the places we had been. He was stationed on an attack troop transport and at many of the islands I had been in the South Pacific. He showed me a picture being home watching the neighborhood youth football team practice. He told me how he got hurt on Tulagi. It was a supply base along with Guadalcanal and Florida Island where my ship was also located. Tulagi was a small, hilly island, that they cut a road through hilly coral. The road was barely wide enough for a truck to get through. They picked up supplies and were going to the dock to unload, but Lou decided to ride on the running board. When going through the pass, it would crush his pelvis that sent him to the base hospital for surgery, then back home for recovery. Our ship would send me on a work crew to get supplies and I would have to go through that same pass, but inside the truck.

Lou would hang out with us at the Hof-Brau until he decided to go to school under the G.I Bill. He stayed close to home and went to Central Connecticut to major in marketing. When he graduated he took a job with a major grocery chain. On a business trips to one of the markets in Stamford he would pay me a visit and take me out to lunch.

Lou had an older brother who joined the Navy in the mid 30's. When he came home on leave, the whole South End was fascinated to see a sailor in uniform. At that time, the flat cap carried the name of the ship you were on. During the war, the ship's name was replaced with U.S Navy.

Lou was not much of a ball player and never played on any of our neighborhood teams. He carried himself as a business executive, which he was. He would see me get into a fight with the neighborhood bully, which I beat the hell out of, and he advised me that I fought so well, why don't I take up professional boxing.

Lou would marry one of the prettiest girls in town and would have three children. His son would die at an early age, and while we were having a few beers one time, he had tears in his eyes and he told me you never get over losing a young child. When we formed the South End Old Timer's Athletic Association, Lou was very helpful to me by organizing our annual awards dinner and helping me give out some awards. Lou would move his family to Florida. He loved to play golf, and you can play there all year long.

Al Gacioch Better Known as "Hack"

This is the last of the neighborhood friends I will write about. Hack also graduated from St. Mary's School and would also leave high school to join the service. He would be assigned to an Infantry Division that fought across France and Into Germany. Hack was quiet in elementary school and never saw much of him in high school. When we got out of the service, we worked for a roofing company with my brother, Ragan. It was tough work, but I would eventually become a construction laborer. Hack would stay with the roofing company until it went out of business. He would then go into factory work from which he retired.

Hack had an older brother named "Ham." He too was drafted into the Army, but lost a leg, not in combat, but from an infection he got playing volleyball. When he got out of the service, he acted like he lost it in combat. He had a bad disposition. When he called you and you didn't come close enough, he'd take his cane, wrap it around your neck, and pull you in. He had a way of starting fights between two other people, and he cheated at playing pinochle. I would tell Hack about the crap his brother pulled, but he'd just shrugged and said he could't do anything about it.

Hack was a good softball player. He played short-stop and when I wasn't catching, I played second base. We were playing a team in Manchester. A double-playball was hit to Hack. I don't know why, but I failed to cover second base. We lost the double-play, which eventually cost us the game. He had the right to chew my ass out, but he just quietly said"Come on, get into the game." He was also a pretty good basketball player and played on our team in the Y.M.C.A. House Basketball League. We would fish together off the Socony Dock, but he loved eels. That's all he fished for, because he would take them home for dinner. If you caught a good sized eel, he would make sure you didn't throw it back, because he wanted him.

Hack had a car and we needed him to drive us to Ted Hilton's. We were there to watch the pretty guests, but all Hack wanted to do was swim. He never got out of the water until it was time to go home. When we retired, Hack would shop for clothing on sale on Main Street. One day, he died of a heart attack in the store.

A Summary Of Struggle And Success

I was too small and lesser skilled to play high school or college varsity sports, but, I held my own while playing softball, football, and basketball on an amateur level. I still carry press releases from the local newspaper highlighting my exceptional moments. We were kids during the Great Depression. I played on our playground team, The Otis Cardinals, in the local city inter-playground league. I made some spectacular catches and game-winning hits, as we won the city playground championships. After the war, we formed a semi-pro football team also named The Otis Cardinals. I still carry a press release highlighting my interception and carrying it for a touchdown that defeated the Waterbury Warriors. But, in a game against The Torrington Indians, I was blindsided in pursuit of a runner that nearly broke my leg and finished my football playing days. Because of injuries, that depleted our team, we had to cancel a game against the inmates of The Connecticut State Prison in Wethersfield.

After working construction for five years after the war, I decided to go to college on the G.I. Bill. I constantly came down with chronic bronchitis infections. While being treated by a local doctor, I told him, in usual idle banter, that I planned to go to the University Of Connecticut. He informed me that, with my chronic pulmonary condition, I needed to go to a school in a warmer climate. I heeded his advice and enrolled at the University Of Florida. Majoring in Physical Education, it was the best decision I ever made, as most classes were held outdoors. I have to mention an incident that happened in our Aquatic Class. The university had the largest, outdoor swimming pool in the country at that time. We were to play the University Of Miami in football that Saturday. Well, inter-collegiate pranks between competing schools are well documented. As we entered the pool for class, a six-foot alligator went wild. It was tossed into our pool by Miami students at night.

Upon graduation, I planned to teach physical education and coach high school football. I was offered positions at rural Florida schools. But my school advisor said that "redneck" schools would not welcome "Yankees." I never really became acclimated to southern culture, so I decided to return home. Even the local students I roomed with would call me a "damned Yankee" but it was a term of endearment. I applied for positions at the schools in my hometown, but found all the positions were filled. It was the same in the surrounding towns. I was a card-carrying laborer, so I decided to write to find a job, and apply to schools the following year. A thought crossed my mind, so I decided to write to the Placement Services at my university. They wrote back saying the Waterbury Y.M.C.A. was looking for a Physical Director. I had a great experience with the Middletown Y.MC.A. as they took us poor kids in during The Depression for Gym And Swim activities without cost. I didn't get the Waterbury job, but they referred me to Stamford, which had an opening. I would interview for the job and get hired. But, I still intended to go into high school coaching. But, "Red "Smith, the Executive Director, was such a fine gentleman, and my Y.M.C.A. experience so rewarding, I would dispense all thoughts of high school coaching, and would stay with the Stamford Y.M.C.A. for 35 years, which was the most satisfying and rewarding position I ever had.

The Stamford Y.M.C.A. was so defunct when I took that position in 1955, that my first gym class had two boys. In those days, you taught the gym class, and then took them to the pool for swim lessons. Eventually our membership grew. We would add a new and larger swimming pool attached to the old building, and with the addition of quality staff, and innovative programming, our membership grew where we needed to build a new and larger Y.M.C.A. The city of Stamford would engage in urban renewal, which attracted many new world corporate headquarters. Their employees would join the Y.M.C.A. and we would be bursting at the seams. I would be promoted to Corporate Fitness Director, which changed the Y.M.C.A. to new program directions. We would add two more Physical and Aquatic Directors to handle the expanding membership. I would develop special testing and training sessions for corporate employees and open the Y.M.C.A. for 7 A.M. and Noon programming. The Y.M.C.A. was filled to capacity all day long. In conjunction with the Stamford Medical Society, we would introduce a cardiac Rehab Exercise Program and Stress Testing, which made us one of the most advanced and forward looking Y.M.C.A.'s in the country. Our varsity basketball and volleyball teams would dominate competition and win State and New England Y.MC.A. Championships. Our boys and girls Y.M.C.A. Swim Teams, under the leadership of Jim Goodridge and John Kandetzki would dominate swim team competitions for years. Our divers would go on to win New England Interscholastic Championships. I would attend certifying workshops in Physical Fitness Testing at Kent State University, Springfield and Hunter College, under Tom Cureton and Ken Cooper, national leaders in Exercise Tests And Measurements. I would introduce these programs at the Y.M.C.A. for corporate employees and the general membership. It was the strong leadership of "Red" Smith, and my staff of Len Rivers, Don Lothrop, and Jim McGrath that made the Stamford Y.M.C.A. one of the most successful and enterprising Y.M.C.A.'s in the country. But, with the retirement of "Red" Smith, whom I would soon follow, the chinks of success began to chip away, as new leadership took over. This leadership was less qualified and made changes that were the antipathy of proven success. Membership faltered because new leadership did not heed the warning and protests of the long-term membership. The death knell was the change in policy of the National Y.M.C.A. Leadership advocating that Y.M.C.A.'s should become one tier membership. The Health Club which provided Executive leadership and corporate financing, would be eliminated, and share a common locker room. Existing leadership called a general meeting of the membership to announce these changes. All the Health Club members attended and voiced disapproval. They were disregarded and left the Y.M.C.A leaving a void that caused it to close. At that meeting, Terry Cooke told them if they let this happen, the

Y.M.C.A. will become "Moribund." He was right as the Y.M.C.A. did close. Health Club members left and joined agencies that still provided Health Club facilities, taking the leadership and financial support that sustained the Y.M.C.A. Because of the exodus, the Y.M.C.A. would close and go out of business. Failing to sell the existing building, they sold the residency that became a private hotel. They decided to reopen the gym, pool, and exercise and locker rooms. Whether they remain in business is questionable, as past membership has moved to other facilities in the community. Reports are that other Y.M.C.A.'s throughout the State have closed. The future of the resurrected Stamford Y.M.C.A. remains questionable.

More "Letters To The Editor"

When Athletes Become Convicts

When the University Of Miami came to play a football game at the University of Notre Dame, the players wore jerseys stating, "Convicts meet the Catholics." There was more reality than connotation as Miami football was noted for renegade behavior. Recent headlines show Aaron Hernandez, a former University of Florida football player, now a star tight end for the New England patriots, being arrested for a possible murder. The victim was a friend of Hernandez, who was suspected of some illegal activity that would implicate him. Two friends of Hernandez were arrested as accomplices. Patriot's Coach Bill Belichick would immediately dismiss Hernandez from the football team, having just signed a $41 million multi year contract. I am an alumnus of the University Of Florida (BSPE, 1955) so I know the history of gator football. Ironically, Hernandez is a native of Bristol, CT. not too far from my hometown, Middletown. After the war, I would play semi-pro football against teams from that town.

While attending U-Fla (1951-1955) football was of poor quality, dominated by Kentucky, Georgia, Auburn, Georgia Tech. But in ensuing years, football got better by hiring top coaches and better recruiting, and would rise to win national championships. Urban Meyer, now coach of Ohio State, was top recruiter, but numerous problems by troubled players would cause him to have a breakdown, and would eventually leave the university. One of those players was Hernandez, but bad publicity about drugs was stifled.

Coach Bill Belichick would draft Hernandez, who would help the Patriots play a number of Super Bowls. But, rumors about drugs and gun incidents circulated, until it exploded into the recent killing that led to the arrest of Hernandez. The big Patriot news was the recent signing of Tim Tebow, a teammate of Hernandez at the University of Florida, but the arrest and his dismissal now dominate the news.

Let me review a time when college football was classical, pure, and noble that reflected the character of the individual and the institution. The Yale Bowl was just 25 miles south of my hometown. In the 30's, I was 10 years old and my brother would take me to the Yale Bowl on Saturday afternoons. Yale football was big time then and the Bowl seated 80,000. We were lucky to get a seat for the Harvard game. The most spectacular sight was to see the Army and Navy Cadet Corps. march into the Bowl at halftime. I saw Yale All Americans Clint Frank and Larry Kelly; Sid Luckman, All American Quarterback from Columbia; and Ray Nitchske, All American linebacker from Pennsylvania. I also saw the deterioration of traditional college football. Yale always defeated UCONN at the Bowl. But in the 80's UCONN upgraded its program and soundly defeated Yale at Storrs. Coach Carm Cozza would terminate playing UCONN stating, 'Yale players are selected by academic index, and we can no longer compete with athletic scholarship programs."

Phil Mushnick, sports columnist for the New York Post (7/1/13) writes that regular college students have become victims of burglaries, hold ups, serious beatings, and even shootings, by criminal athletes recruited to play football or basketball. ESPN college basketball analyst, Jay Bilas, once reasoned that even if scholarship athletes do not attend classes, their social skills improve by their mere presence in a college environment. A stupefying remark made by a former Duke basketball player who was a member of a national championship team coached by Mike Krzyewski considered one of the cleanest programs in the country. Prodigious TV money is causing educational institutions to look the other way. They will eventually destroy themselves by greed and lack of control.

A Church Gone Astray

There have been many reports in the past where Bishops turned a blind eye to the sexual abuse of children by Priests under their jurisdiction. Many of these offenders were sent to other parishes, or to a rehab center that was ineffective. This is not a church in crisis, but a church in self-destruction. Father Brett, the most notorious offender, would flee to the islands to escape prosecution. The hand of God would extract justice as Father Brett was found dead after falling down a flight of stairs. Father DeVore, pastor of my church, would secretly communicate with him, and when found out, would be forced to resign and do penance. Fairfield County Diocese is replete with wayward priests. Father Jude Fay of St. John's of Noroton, and Father Michael Moynihan of St, Michael's in Greenwich, would cohabitate with their lovers right in the rectory, plus steal over one million dollars in church funds. Throw in the latest Of Father Kevin Wallin (Advocate 1/23/13) who staged cross-dressing bashes right in the rectory, and you have a trifecta. The most notorious incident was Father Madden being punished for exposing the romps and thefts of Father Jude Fay. Bishop Lori forced Father Madden to write a letter of apology and sent to Siberia to do penance. Father Madden would resign from the priesthood saying," Something inside of me died when I was forced to sign that letter. It mutilated my spirit and crushed my vocation."

I once read how a professor at the Evangelical Fuller Theological Seminary in Pasadena, California told his class that anyone who did not refer to God in the feminine would be given a failing grade. God would react to this as He did with the San Hedrin, calling them whited sepulchers full of dead man's bones. Jesus foresaw the deviancy that would infiltrate His growing church. You will find it in one of His profound sayings," When the Son Of Man comes, will He find faith left on Earth?" Do you know, before Bishop Lori fled to Baltimore, he spent over one million dollars of Sunday collection money on an elite legal team, trying to suppress a press release, divulging the millions of dollars paid out to sexual abuse victims of his diocese? The Supreme Court sent him home whimpering.

When Lobbying Rules

Legislation for the ban of assault weapons, prompted by the massacre of teachers and children at Sandy Hook School, was defeated by heavy lobbying by the National Rifle Association. I would like to see the amount donated to the legislators who voted against the ban. The father of one of the slain children would certainly proclaim, "I am ashamed to see that Congress doesn't have the guts to stand up and make a change." Do you know, newly elected members of Congress are usually $200,000 a year lawyers who, after a six-year term, become millionaires? Want to know why? It is due to the bountiful lobbying funds they are given, which trumps legislative courage. Let me cite some figures: lobbyists outnumber Congress 130-1. They spent $28.6 billion on lobbying compared to $492 million for labor, a 60-1 business advantage. The political insiders are the 'new power game' in Washington, dominated by well-financed professional lobbyists. Many of them are former members of Congress, and government officials with an inside track, working for special interests like Wall Street, banks, the oil, defense and pharmaceutical industries and business trade associations. Dick Cheney's Haliburton Enterprises, needing no congressional clearance, was the biggest supplier for the Gulf wars totaled in the billions with little public accounting. In a recent TV interview, he was defiant, arrogant, and evasive, mocking the TV interviewers, which is indicative of our wealthy, powerful politicians. We have also seen this with Chris Dodd and Charles Rangel.

The Governor's Proposed Budget Cuts Awaken Memories

One of Governor Dannell Malloy's proposed budget cuts is the elimination of the Connecticut Valley Hospital Fire Department located in my former hometown of Middletown. While I was growing up, it was named the Connecticut State Asylum, a huge campus situated on a hill overlooking the Connecticut River. It was the state's central treatment center for the mentally ill.

The whole asylum was originally secured, encircled by a six-foot high fence of sharpened cast iron bars. The entrance gate was the only opening manned by a guard. All the wards had barred windows and screened porches from which you heard screaming, yelling, cursing and crying. The most interesting section of the asylum was the facility for the criminally insane. For exercise, they were led into a circular, heavily barred courtyard we called the 'bullpen." When we were kids, we would gain access to the grounds through the open farmland. We would observe them, some in strait jackets, others performing weird acts of behavior, hoping they would never escape. It still exists.

They grew all their vegetables and raised livestock: pigs, cows, and chickens. Sometimes we would play" wiseacres," go where the pigs were grazing, and yell," Sooiee!! Sooiee!! Pig, pig, pig!!" In a stampede, they would come running and squealing, thinking the call was feeding time. We had to jump the fence to keep from being trampled.

It all changed in the 1960's. Mental Health advocates convinced the courts that treatment should be community based in group homes. When you walked down Main Street, you would encounter groups of released patients, straggling, disheveled, with little sense of where they were. Even the supervisors were indistinguishable. Since this happened, all fences have been removed. The unoccupied buildings, unused for years, fell into disrepair and were demolished.

New buildings were constructed and are now mainly drug detoxification centers. The locals now call the facility a "junkie haven."

That institution has made my former hometown groan in agony many times. One escapee set many downtown buildings on fire, including the church of my youth, built by Polish immigrants. It was totally destroyed, including irreplaceable stained glass windows imported from France. Another patient would rape and murder a therapist in an isolated treatment area. A local church group is petitioning the state for the release into their custody, a patient who killed his wife with a baseball bat. By far, the most agonizing incident happened when a patient made it downtown, purchased a knife at a hardware store, and slashed to death a ten-year-old girl.

My former hometown was also the site, since abandoned, for the Connecticut Reform School for Delinquent Girls, formerly named Long Lane. Under much opposition, the state has recently constructed a $50 million detention center for delinquent boys. Furor has been constant. The former scandal sheet (Bridgeport Herald) had dubbed Middletown the "Dumping Grounds." The weight of history and emotional wreckage of tragedy rest heavy on my mind. If you can spare a week, ask me about it.

Permanent Political Class

Thomas Sowell, New York Post columnist, writes in his article (10/31/13) how career politicians have become the "New Permanent Ruling Class." The rise of the permanent political class in Washington came with the rise of the vast government apparatus with unprecedented amounts of money and power to control and corrupt individuals, institutions, and the fabric of the whole society. Years ago, a proposal was made to restrict government service to two, six-year terms, just as the presidency was restricted to two, four-year terms. The sitting Congress soundly defeated it.

The founding fathers were not career politicians. They served one, six-year term, then returned to their home states to resume their lives as private citizens. There are now people in Washington whose entire adult lives have been spent in government. Turnover in Congress has been reduced almost to a vanishing point. A point was made in a recent article that many legislators were $200,000 a year lawyers. After one, six-year term, they are now millionaires. Thomas Sowell suggests the first step in limiting and then scaling back government itself must be limiting the time that anyone can remain in office-preferably to one term, to make it harder to become career politicians, a species we can well do without.

It all started during George Washington's presidency, during his second term. With the creation of the two party system and their constant bickering, he became so frustrated; he refused to run a third term. He said, "the parties are so agitating, they can nominate a broomstick, and get it elected."

Why Bullying Persists

The Advocate (8/29/13) highlights the suicide of a Greenwich High School student due to bullying he endured. There has been a steady stream of reporting of bullying suicides in local newspapers across the country. This newspaper would print (5/5/10) a report I wrote on my past experiences with school and World War II U.S. Navy bullies I encountered and how they were resolved. Even President Obama would call a national conference (1/12/12) to stem the unabated incidents of student suicides due to bullying.

Do you know why school bullying goes unabated in our schools? Because of the lack of strong enforceable actions of school administrators and boards of education. I wrote in this newspaper (5/5/2013) how we handled bullies in my school days (1939-43), and aboard ship during WWII; how my son would handle a bully menacing his kid sister in our local high school; and how I am teaching my grandchildren to handle bullies they encounter in their schools.

I would inquire of local school officials as to how they manage bullying. They have an administrative process that is commendable, but is circumvented by clever tactics of bullies, or aggressive parental interference.

School bullying has been ongoing since our educational system originated, but pioneering children, reared in difficult times, would engage the bully toe to toe. Attending school during the Great Depression would toughen children to take on a bully.

The fact is bullies are everywhere: in business, in politics, in government, in law enforcement, in the armed service. It is the timid who are the victims. It is a hard lesson, but the tough fight back. There are examples of tough kids engaging bullies, but a line has been drawn by threatened litigation. Will it come to challenging the legal profession to an alley fight?

America Today

The book, <u>Who Stole The American Dream</u> by Hedrick Smith, tells of the rise and demise of the middle class in America. It starts at a time when I was born in 1925. It was a time when America was comprised of two classes: the rich and the "masses." There was no economic quagmire than the Great Depression of the 1930's. Survival depended on soup and bread lines, and agricultural surplus handouts. World War II would enliven the economy with war production while we marched off to war. When the Veterans came home, the G.I. Bill would offer educational opportunities to become professional teachers, lawyers, engineers, accountants, scientists, etc. That saw the rise of the middle class in the 1950's, 60's and 70's with professional careers offering the American Dream of a steady job with decent pay and health benefits, rising living standards, secure retirement, and hope that your children would enjoy a better future.

Since the 70's, the soaring wealth of the super rich brought the unraveling of the American Dream for the middle class. The political insiders are the "new power game" in Washington, dominated by well financed professional lobbyists, many of them former members of Congress and government officials with an inside track, working for special interests like Wall Street, banks, oil, defense, and pharmaceutical industries and business trade associations. Lobbyists out number Congress 130-1. They spent $28.6 billion on lobbying compared to $492 million for labor, a 60-1 business advantage. Dick Cheney's Haliburton Enterprises, needing no congressional clearance, was the biggest supplier for the Gulf wars totaled in the billions with very little public accounting.

The shifts of power and wealth have led to the unraveling American Dream for the middle class, leaving them with little impact on public policy and less connected to government and our governing officials. I would advise you to read Hedrick Smith's book as he outlines how we might, through changed policies and revival of citizens' action, restore our unity and reclaim the American Dream for the average citizen.

Watch For Hilary

Novels can be a great window into the human condition, but reality casts no shadows. Today's news features the stumbling of President Obama on our new national healthcare plan. Today we are getting a glimpse of when God is cast out, and man takes His place. A conglomerate of celebrities takes over, entertainers, athletes, and politicians.

Obama was a typical Chicago politician, rubbing elbows with former Gov. Rod Blagojevich, now in prison for trying to sell a Senate seat, firebrand Rev. Jeremiah Wright preaching "kill Whitey," Tony Rezko, crooked real estate dealer doing prison time, and Bill Ayers, bomb planting Hippie, who escaped prosecution. When asked about his association with these rascals, Obama contended it was a "bonehead move."

Having arrived in Washington without past or a well defined personality, (except the golden gift of oratory); he mysteriously bumped Hilary Clinton, who was a shoo-in for the presidency. But, when you change the public image of a leader, you change history. Obama would appoint Hilary as Secretary Of State, who served an undistinguished career. Her greatest failure was denying any role in the Benghazi killings. She would aggravate that failure by angrily shouting during a Senate hearing, "What difference does it make?"

She resigned from her office of Secretary Of State, and is now contemplating to once again run for the Presidency, stolen by Obama. This is how people lose contact with their own traditional strength and virtues then climb that hill again to regain her lost honor. She stretches the limits of political forbearance, which has silver bullet consequences.

Angela Carella – No Frills Reporter

In an Advocate article (10/25/13), Angela Carella writes about Michael Skakel's latest appeal for another trial in his murder conviction of Martha Moxley in Greenwich in 1975. I have followed all of her articles, especially corruption in various Stamford departments. Her reporting is straight and factual, and avoids all intent of self-gratification. She disdains the fact twisting and truth bending of other high-indexed national newspapers.

She follows the dogma: truth in journalism adhered to by the editor of the New Hampshire Guardian (1926):"The Primary office of a newspaper is the gathering of news. Loyalty to the truth must be uncompromising." The old Chicago City News Bureau held fast to the adage: "If your mother tells you she loves you, check it out."

Whatever she writes is authentic and fact based. I was interviewed by her (6/2/2013) concerning my first published book, "A Voice In The Village Square"; a compilation of my letters to the editor, mainly concerning local, state, and national politics as well as church pedophile scandals. I was scheduled to have a book signing at Borders, but the bookstore closed before it took place. I tried to reschedule at Barnes and Noble, but I was told, "Get away kid, you bother me."

My book also contained an article I wrote summarizing Skakel's murder conviction.

The old Bridgeport Herald was the prince of scandal reporting, matching the cigar smoke haze of the back room Chicago reporting. President Barack Obama is a product of Chicago's back room politics. President Obama would have an array of radical and criminal associates in his Chicago days: radical preacher Jeremiah Wright, 60's hippie terrorist and bomb planting Bill Ayers, imprisoned real estate dealer Tony Rezko, and also serving the former Governor, Rod Blagojevich. President Obama brushes all this off as a "bonehead move."

Angela Carella rises above them all. When you pan for gold, she is the nugget that makes you smile. Mr. Editor, don't lose her.

Dumbing Down Presidential Elections

George Will, noted syndicated columnist (9/20) chides President Obama and challenger Mitt Romney for their grade school responses to the recent outbreak of violence in the Middle East. "It would require exquisitely precise intellectual calipers to gauge which idea is silliest," writes Will. He states, "Many voters will be astonished by, and even be grateful for the novelty of being addressed as adults." In life, especially in our politics of past presidents (Nixon, Carter, Clinton, and the Bushes) has led to the erosion of the rhythms of life. They all remind me of the definition of an appeaser: one who feeds the crocodile hoping it will eat him last. They all tinker around the edges because they lack the prism of truth. Both Obama and Romney lack the maturity required to be prophetic or profound. When they speak, they give us slippery platitudes. After Richard Nixon was elected President, he was asked why he hadn't fulfilled all his presidential promises. He responded, "They were all campaign rhetoric." Yet there was no outcry by the voting public. Why is there no authoritative, received truth that restrains this in our government? Just what has become the core tenet of democracy? In debate, when a President mesmerizes the public with his musical oratory, fabricated for political purposes that have no basis in reality, the public pulpits grow silent. We as a nation have become unhinged with a chill inducing national debt, two long-term wars, high unemployment, and a shaky economy. We need a president who will reclaim the ordinance of "We the people" as prescribed by our Founding Fathers; to bond together in triumph of the human spirit. How long must we wait?

Memories Of A Valiant Ship

It was interesting to read the article, "New Pearl Harbor Memorial Bridge Dedicated" (Advocate 6/24), and the comments made by some Navy Veterans in attendance. Jack Stoeber of Milford, who was stationed aboard the USS Whitney on December 7, 1941, commented how he manned an anti aircraft gun during the attack. I was 15 at the time, but joined the Navy when I turned 17, and would board the USS Whitney at Noumea, New Caledonia and head for Guadalcanal. We would follow the invasion forces as they progressed up the Solomons, onto New Guinea, the Admiralty Islands, and finally the Philippines. In the Admirality Islands, A Japanese Suicide submarine (a Kaiten) snuck into the harbor and blew up the ammunition ship the USS Mount Hood. The fireball was such a huge cauldron that no trace of the ship or the crew was ever found. Damage to ships within half a mile was indescribable. I would later learn that five friends of mine from my hometown were lost with that ship. We were in Leyte Gulf when the war ended, gearing up to join the occupation forces in Tokyo Bay. Veteran crew were given the option to stay with the ship or head home. Don't even ask what choice I made. The Whitney returned stateside after a year, then was stricken from the rolls and scrapped.

Nuns Under Siege

In a recent article in the September issue of Connecticut Magazine, the Vatican crackdown of American Nuns, especially the Leadership Conference on Women's Religious (LCWR) is a surprising and revealing harsh judgment. The Congregation for the Doctrine Of The Faith (CDF) once the office of the inquisition, accuses the LCWR of promoting radical feminist themes; gay marriage, contraception, abortion, ordination of women. Many of theses nuns are part of the community living at the Villa Notre Dame in Wilton. They work in the most rundown sections of Bridgeport, caring for poor mothers with children, mostly immigrant and Hispanic. Their harshest critics are Bishop Law and Bishop Lori. Both were involved in covering up for pedophile priests. Law was forced to resign, while Lori was backhanded by the U.S. Supreme Court after spending over one million dollars of Sunday collections to suppress court ordered payouts. Both should have been called to account by their superiors in Rome. But, Rome became an accessory by rewarding them with promotions. Yet, Lori and Law have petitioned the CDF to launch an investigation into the LCWR.

In a recent shocker (NY Daily News, 8/31), well-known and highly respected Rev. Benedict Groeschel came to the defense of convicted pedophile, Jerry Sandusky, stating that the kids are to blame. David Clohessy, director of the supervisors' network of those abused by priests, called Father Groeschel's remarks, "Disgusting." Joseph Zwillling, spokesman for the New York Archdiocese condemned Groeschel's statement as "terribly wrong." Rome should bring the hammer down on Father Groeschel, and leave the nuns alone.

I am the product of a Polish parochial school taught by the Felician Order during the Great Depression. Central to their teaching was to adhere to the words of Christ. And from the pulpit on Sunday was the admonition of sin. When was the last time you heard "sin" mentioned in a Sunday sermon?

The nuns have held discussions with delegates from Rome, but are resistant to their mandate, "We'll talk, you listen." There is a stalemate to this issue, and the Pope may have to resolve it. The original twelve were not installed with unchallenged authority. Nor were their successors vested with it. But watch out for spunky nuns who discarded their habits because it made them feel like penguins.

A Garland In The Garrison

Open homosexuality in the armed services has always been proscribed. The recent repeal of, "Don't ask, don't tell" is yet to be propitiated. It is an opus that the premise of tolerance and equality is wholesome and refreshing. We have heard from the top that this will be a gilding for the grunts who face enemy fire "outside the wire," perhaps in officer's quarters, where life is discreet. But what about amongst the troops in the trenches, and in close quarters of the barracks? This is a discretionary entitlement for "gays" with no serious regard to merit or consequences. If recruitment is stifled, it has dire implications in the ranks, as it will put the entire military on life support.

Syndicated columnist Cal Thomas, and Sen. John McCain (Arizona) warn that this repeal will cause an alarming troop retention problem as large numbers of personnel will quit or retire. The president and his cadre of poseurs need to be reminded that the constitution defines and limits their powers. That the polemical assumption that abnormality is morally neutral is harmful. Most Americans today never had a military experience, therefore cannot comprehend the consequences of "don't ask, don't tell." But the fire of public argument is smoldering, and when full realization is stoked, the crucible of opposition will be forged.

There has been a scattering of reports in some newspapers from high-ranking officers and enlisted personnel to their opposition to the repeal. I would venture to say they are expressing the will of the majority. When does the Pentagon start ordering pink curtains?

Genuflect To Celebrity

To the Editor:

When the sun comes up, spiders leave their web and seek prey. When the sun goes down, the spiders of the entertainment world seek out each other to devour a critical public.

The saintly Liz Taylor schmooze's with the fallen Michael Jackson (still dressed for Halloween), and inveighs the accusations of child molestation (again). And the legions of Michael's followers here and abroad, cry out for the blood of the accuser, a cancer stricken child. Bordering on worship and bereft of reason, they are frenzy driven.

Perverted loyalty makes all subsequent actions paltry. We have seen this before: O. J., the Clinton's, P. Diddy. And, today, we are seeking it in Kobe Bryant. Celebrity is revered, but the accuser is deemed a ghoul.

Hollywood, the Rappers, Rock and Rollers, assault us with impunity with their words, their actions, their dress, and their lifestyle. They get away with it and grow bolder because the vast majority of good people do nothing, and expire in their silence.

We can learn from crows. During the change in seasons, a large congregation assembles in the deep forest; raucously berate the transgressor whose behavior endangers the flock, and one by one peck out his feathers. Why are the animals smarter than we?

When The Nation Mourned Fallen Presidents

I was working at the YMCA when the news of the assassination of President John F. Kennedy was announced on November 22, 1963. A solemn and sad atmosphere enveloped the whole nation. The whole country would gather around their television sets to view reports of the circumstances leading up to the assassination. The country came to a halt to view the funeral procession and internment at Arlington National Cemetery. Who can forget Jacqueline Kennedy, dressed in mournful black, telling little John, John to salute his father's caisson as it passed by. There were two other presidents whose funerals were held when the nation was at war.

I was a young sailor, just 18 years old, aboard ship in the Leyte Gulf in the Philippines. Okinawa was just secured and the naval forces were gearing up for the invasion of the Japanese mainland. It was April of 1945 when the news reached us that President Franklin Delano Roosevelt had passed away. I was on duty as the ship's messenger standing guard with the officer of the deck at the forward gangway at the time. It was my duty to raise the union jack at the ship's bow, simultaneously with the raising of the flag. They both had to be lowered at half-mast for 30 days. Vice President Harry Truman would automatically resume the presidency. When given a report as to the amount of casualties we would incur in the invasion of the Japanese mainland, he gave the order to drop the atom bomb. The estimated casualties were so great; it would make D-Day and Iwo Jima seem like minor skirmishes.

The assassination of President Abraham Lincoln had greater negative and undesirable consequences for the nation than Roosevelt and Kennedy. When Lee surrendered to Grant, Lincoln proposed freed slaves be given 40 acres and a mule, giving them the opportunity to become entrepreneurs. They would integrate into American society and have the same opportunities for economic, social, educational and political advancement. But with Lincoln's assassination, the South seized the opportunity to curtail Lincoln's proposals, and would set back integration that still exists today. I would feel the sting of Southern recalcitration while attending the University Of Florida on the G.I. Bill, enduring four years of taunts, "You damn Yankee, we whopped your ass." That still stings in my fading memory.

A Call For A Third Party

In Mark Drought's opinion piece, "It's Time To Throw The Bums Out-All Of Them" (Advocate, 12/9/11), he bemoans the failure of democracy, citing the latest Washington debacle, the failure of the deficit-reduction of the super committee. He goes on to say that both parties care more about ideology than fiscal responsibility and have chosen partisanship over patriotism. He calls this "uncompromising extremism" that makes responsible governing impossible. He suggests a solution by calling for a third party for the upcoming 2012 elections.

Our country has a long history of third parties. The first third party candidate appeared in the 1808 election won by James Madison. George Clinton of New York ran on the Independent Party gathering 6 electoral votes. In 1848, Martin van Buren would run on the Free Soil Party getting 200,000 votes. Abraham Lincoln would win the 1860 election with 1.8 million votes, but was hard pressed by the third party candidate Democrat Stephen Douglas who received 1.3 million votes. Eugene Debs would run under the Socialist banner in 1908, 1912, and 1916.

The biggest third party vote getters would be George Wallace (American Independent) with 10 million popular votes and 46 electoral votes. Ross Perot ran under the Independent ticket in 1992 against Bill Clinton. He gathered close to 20 million votes. Others trying to crash the party, J. Strom Thurman under the States Rights Party, better known as "Dixiecrats" Jesse Jackson with his Rainbow coalition, and Ralph Nader and the Green Party. The 2000 election proved to be the most controversial since the United States Supreme Court had to decide the winner. Al Gore would complain Nader's votes deprived him of the Presidency.

The most recent development is a group of Wesleyan Grads calling themselves "Unity 2008", have banded together to advocate a third party to challenge the long, dominant two parties in power. They feel the honorable call to politics, to make the right decisions for the common good, has been vaporized by inter-party fratricide. They claim when government becomes so big as to become beyond the consent of the governed, you reap unashamed corruption and trillion dollar deficits. Based on the premise that all citizens have reasonable expectations that the people they elect will transcribe the will of the people, they have set out on a course of change. Fed up with the ugly, unproductive partisan warfare, "Unity 2008" is determined to rise up and do something about it. Refreshing, isn't it?

The Lore Of The Crow

My yard and neighborhood has been inundated by large gatherings of crows. Their numbers have multiplied ten-fold and have become a nuisance and a curiosity. They fill the treetops, roofs, and cover the ground pecking and feeding. They are not easily disturbed and only take flight when approached. I grew up along the Connecticut River and have a long history with crows, sometimes compatible and sometimes nemesis.

Growing up during the Depression, we all hunted game to supplement the dinner table. Wild ducks, pheasants, partridge, rabbits and squirrels were plentiful. Crows were everywhere, but considered a nuisance. They were wary and cagey, and very adept at keeping themselves out of harm's way. The flock protected themselves by placing a lone sentry at a safe distance who would sound the alarm as hunters approached. Then, the flock would break out in a cawing ruckus that agitated both humans and animals. This agitation was the only reason we would try to bring them down, since they were inedible.

Lore has it, that in late fall, a very large number of crows would gather deep in the forest to hold court. Judgment was to be passed on a lone member who transgressed against the code of behavior. If found guilty, the flock would descend on the perpetrator, peck his eyes and most of his feathers out in a clawing frenzy, then would turn the sky black as they dispersed in silence.

It is impossible for anyone to have never encountered a crow or two. I don't know the number that has crossed your path, but match that number to this following ditty: "One is for bad news; Two is for mirth; Three is a wedding; Four is for birth; Five is for riches; Six is a thief; Seven is a journey; Eight is for grief; Nine is a secret; Ten is for sorrow; Eleven is for love; Twelve is for joy tomorrow."

Robert Burns, the Scottish poet writes, "My Mary's asleep by thy murmuring stream. Flow gently sweet Afton, disturb not her dream." I do not know if crows inhabit the banks of the River Afton, but I can visualize the tempest of ire of this great poet, if cranky crows gather there.

Tulip Eating Deer

To the Editor:

During a harsh winter, deer regularly enter my back yard to feed on acorns I leave for the squirrels. Every few years, my huge oak tree is endowed with double the normal yield of acorns. The squirrels knock most of them down, and I find it impossible to rake them all up. Now I'm happy to provide these critters with sustenance during difficult winters, but the deer overstay their welcome.

As Spring approaches, and the crocus and snowbells peek from the snow, I daily check for the first shoots of my tulips and daffodils. I am heartened as they inch upward. After reaching about four inches, they suddenly disappear. All that is left is stubble at ground level. The crocuses are nibbled away also.

At first, I blamed other animals, but upon close scrutiny, I find deer tracks in the soft sod.

Now I've had my garden trampled by my grandchildren as a ball goes astray during play. I don't get mad, but I softly admonish them to be more careful. Can anyone tell me how to keep my composure with the deer? Shooting in not an option.

I raise my flowers to give away, but I am being denied an act of generosity. The Gospel is steeped with the need for forgiveness. Can an animal be forgiven?

Schoolyard Justice For Bullies

Pabulum treatment is making bullying a national crisis. Lacking a forceful response to bullying from school authorities, student suicides continue. The latest was a 15-year-old girl in New York City who was so tormented that she committed suicide by throwing herself under a bus.

School bullying has gone unchallenged for so long that it has become deadly and expansive. President Barack Obama called a national conference at the White House to explore the issue and seek solutions. I had expected the president to be forceful and decisive: issuing directives to all bullies to halt their fear inducements or the consequences will be swift and compelling. Instead, he was full of mushy lamentations ("Bullying is not a rite of passage.")

I wrote in this newspaper (Opinion, Feb. 5, 2010) about how determined neighborhood kids had the resiliency and courage to solve a schoolyard problem; and of my experience with a bully 65 years ago, and how he was schooled in proper behavior.

My eldest son, "Casey," 35 years later, would teach a bully menacing his kid sister right here in one of our local schools the principles of effacement. In the Navy, during World War II, I would engage the ship's bully on the fantail and drop anchor on him. As seen above, that family practice continues.

We are seeing a proliferation of anti-bullying advocates, publishing and lecturing to school assemblies with proven guidelines to eliminate the plague. To me, their proposals and recommendations are the equivalent of David bringing down Goliath with a marshmallow.

Restraining bullies is not a choice, but a duty. Steely grit trumps timidity.

Why is this so hard to comprehend? You can't talk a bully down any more than you can talk a cat down from a tree. The bully must be made to feel the sting he administers. This is his/her adjudication. My first grade and kindergarten grandchildren are being taught to strip the bark off bullies they encounter.

Call me a dinosaur, but do not question its effectiveness.

THE RISE AND ENSUING
FALL OF AMERICA

America was built on self-reliance and unwavering courage, to cast off the rule of a British monarchy. Rules of conduct were standard, and loyalty to country a badge of honor. Democracy was born, and it still struggles with growing pains. The country grew as the move westward added more territory, but uprooted the Native Americans from their land, and confined them to reservations. The gold strike would open the West to greater expansion. But the conflicts over slavery plunged the nation into Civil War that nearly destroyed a fledgling democracy. President Lincoln devised a solution to assimilate former slaves into our society, but his assassination allowed the South to stifle Lincoln's proposal, setting back the nation's slavery solution that has yet to fully resolve to this day. The nation grew, and we would play a minor role during World War I. The treachery of Japan attacking Pearl Harbor would force us to declare war on Japan and Germany. We would mobilize and engage the enemy in Europe and the Pacific. Our superior war production, and the creation of the Atom Bomb, would end both wars from which we would emerge as the strongest country in the world. Our ally in that war, the Soviet Union, would turn against us, leaving the threat of World War III. They would suddenly disintegrate as a threatening world power, but open the door for Islam to rise and be the next threat to world stability, hijacking our aircraft and knocking down out twin towers on 9/11. It would lead into warfare with Iraq and Afghanistan that has prolonged over ten years, that is causing our nation to demand we withdraw from these conflicts. Since the main objective has been accomplished, the death of Osama Bin Laden, negotiations are underway to withdraw from both countries. Politics has engendered into a costly and corrupt process. The Founding Fathers chose to serve one or two terms then return home. It has now become lifetime tenure so profligate and profitable, that we as a nation are now engulfed in a trillion dollar deficit. The proliferation of personal billionaires and the cresting of the middle class may be the beginning of the end of democracy.

THE SPIRIT OF DEMOCRACY AND THE THREAT OF ELITISM

In the New Oxford Review, Robert Lowry Clinton, Professor and Chair Emeritus in the Department of Political Science at Southern Illinois University, writes how his friend and mentor, Wallace Mendleson states, "No man is fit to govern another" In that simple and true statement is contained the whole spirit of Democracy. He suggests that Democracy is, in some sense, a moral requirement., not merely a political form. Democracy is still an experiment, and like all experiments is fraught with danger. John Adams said two centuries ago, "Democracy never lasts long. It soon wastes, exhausts and murders itself. There never was a Democracy that did not commit suicide." G.K.Chesterton once asked, "Why are governments of the world morally defective?" He answers, "Moral decency in government is so rare, that even the most Democratic regimes of modernity, forces are constantly at work to undermine its underlying principle that men ought to be allowed some meaningful say in the decisions that determine how they are to live their lives". Jean Jacques Rousseau rightly observed, the forces of the corporate will (the interest of government or the ruling elite) are always busy undermining the general will (the common good) the elimination of prayer in the classroom, same sex marriage, political correctness, etc. Why are these forces constantly at work? Because power corrupts, not sometimes, but always; not because they are vicious or inept, but because governing others always, in the last analysis, requires more virtue that any man can muster.

Fallen human nature ensures that those who wield power will always succumb to pride. They will forget the maxim that no man is fit to govern another. They will be on the road to elitism. The deep truths of Democracy, that no man is really fit to govern another, and that people ought to have a meaningful say in the decisions that determine how they live, give the lie to all utopian political schemes. They are the reason why

69

government must be limited, balanced, and controlled. The U.S. Constitution was a good start in this effort, but it has been eroded in the past century, and seems under even more serious threat today. What is developing is the worshipful attitude toward science and technology, an attitude that those possessing scientific expertise to affect public policy, is the eugenics movement. Influential scientific elites are able to enshrine a secular orthodoxy in policy making process. The purpose to diminish the influence of religion in the public square, and substituting a materialistic public philosophy masquerading as science. On this topic, Chesterton warned, "Once abolish the God, and the government becomes the God". This is why scientism is fatal to Democracy. Eric Voegelin calls it, "the dehumanizing of man". Another grave threat to our democracy involves the moneyed establishment. In 2008 and 2009, elites in the financial community, and their allies in government, provoked the largest economic crisis since the great depression; crisis that enriched the lavish lifestyle of a few, while giving evidence of wanton and callous disregard for ordinary stockholders, pensioners and others. Mike Lofgren charged," The super-rich with having seceded from America, and their grip on power has tightened". That grip has tightened largely because the growing influence of money; made clear in the ever escalating cost of political campaigns, and the virtual impossibility of advancement to high office by anyone who is not supported by those with substantial wealth. Billionaires now rule. Millionaires are common. Long ago, Aristotle warned that too much or too little - wealth is dangerous to human flourishing. There has become a "disconnect" between ordinary citizens and their elected leaders. A distinctive culture has emerged in and around our nation's capitol that has isolated the super wealthy from the rest of the country. James Madison explained on behalf of the Founding Fathers, "An elective despotism is not the government we fought for". There is a great danger to Democracy in the progressive elites now governing, who are convinced they know best how the rest of us should conduct our lives, have enacted policies in apparent disregard of public opinion and traditional American values and principles. Among these policies are government run health care, government bailout of failed corporations, efforts to defeat state and local initiatives to control border security, refusal to enforce the defense of the marriage act, and spearheaded by the First Lady to determine what we eat. Even Chief Supreme Court Justice Roberts reversed his initial position on the affordable care act on the law's unconstitutionality due to his fear of an assault on the Court's legitimacy by the nation's elite. All the threats to our Constitutional Democracy are rooted in elitism, the belief or conviction that ordinary people are not really fit to govern themselves, and small groups of people "in the know"- whether scientific, technological, economic, political, legal, or academic elites – can do a better job and are therefore entitled to do the governing for us. The trouble is, if the elitist assumption is true, then the deep truths of Democracy that no man is really fit to govern another, and that people ought to have a meaningful say in the decisions that determine how they live, are necessarily false. While Barack Obama was an Illinois senator in 2001, he criticized the Warren Court for not breaking free "from the essential constraints that were placed by the founding fathers in the Constitution."

Days Gone By

When life was like a story,
holding neither sob nor sigh,
in the olden, golden glory of,
the days gone by.

James Whitmore Riley

Photo History Of
The Gawlak Family

THE FAMILY GROWS UP

WHEN CATS BECOME FAMILY

HAPPY TIMES

HAPPY GRANDCHILDREN

GRANDMA AND GRANDPA

THIS I WILL REMEMBER,

WHEN THE REST OF MY LIFE

IS THROUGH,

THE FINEST THING I'VE EVER

DONE,

IS SIMPLY LOVING YOU.

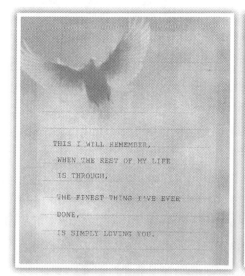

WHEN MY CAPS BECAME APPEALING

SPECIAL MOMENTS WITH THE GRANDCHILDREN

GRAM AND GRAMPS JOIN THE GRANDCHILDREN

WHEN SMILES INDICATE HAPPINESS

FAMILY GET-TOGETHERS

WEDDING BELLS ARE BREAKING UP THAT OLD GANG OF MINE

FISHING WITH FAMILY AND FRIENDS BRINGS A TOUCH OF HAPPINESS

A REQUIEM

FOR ALL SAILORS WHO LIE IN THE DEEP

Waste no time grieving...for I am still with you, but in a different venue. My love for you is deeper than the ocean where I now abide...Come sit by the sea and talk to me...if I recognize your voice, I will answer. And if your love for me has been true...You will always see me in the Summer surf...the Autumn sky...and in the Winter spray...When you visit me by the side of the sea...gaze out over the horizon...There you will find me walking with Him, who bids the storm to be still.